The Rat Hunt

written by Jenny Alexander
illustrated by Jenny Mumford

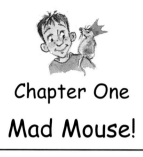

Chapter One

Mad Mouse!

Mouse and Jojo were so excited, they could hardly eat their breakfast. The table was covered with birthday presents, and all they wanted to do was play with them.

Mum was putting the finishing touches to the cake, and Pip wanted to help. She gave him a chocolate curl and told him to go and get ready for school. "You'd better get a move on too," she told Jojo and Mouse.

They went upstairs. Mouse put Ricky gently into his cage, and plumped up his paper bedding. "Have a good long sleep while I'm at school," Mouse told him. "Because when I get back, it'll be party time!"

Jojo laughed. "What does he care about party time?" she said. Mouse turned round.

"Ricky loves parties. They have lots of his favourite thing in the world – food!"

"If you think I'm letting that rat come to my party tea, you must be mad!" Jojo exclaimed.

"It's my party too!" said Mouse.

Chapter Two

A Bad Start

Mouse and Jojo were so excited about their party, they could hardly concentrate on their school work. The day seemed to go on forever. When at last the school bell rang, they shot out of the classroom and ran all the way home.

The house looked fantastic. There were bunches
of balloons all over the place, and Pip had made
a banner.

The table was piled high with wonderful food.
   "Wait until Ricky sees this!" Mouse exclaimed.

Mouse raced up the stairs and went into his bedroom. But then he stopped short. The cage door was open, and Ricky was nowhere to be seen.

Mouse thought he knew what had happened. He was furious. He went straight back downstairs and grabbed Jojo by the sleeve. "You let him out, didn't you? You didn't want him at the party!"

Jojo was speechless. She had no idea what he was talking about. Mrs Macdonald told Mouse to let go of his sister and explain himself. "She let Ricky out of his cage, and now I've lost him," Mouse wailed.

Mrs Macdonald turned to Jojo. "Is this true?" she asked.

"Of course not!" said Jojo. "He must have forgotten to shut the door properly this morning."

"She's lying!" shouted Mouse.

Their mother suggested that they stop arguing and start searching. Ricky couldn't have gone far.

The whole family joined in the search for Ricky. But they still hadn't found him when their friends started arriving for the party. Jojo let them in. She yelled up the stairs to Mouse. She was dying to open her presents.

But Mouse didn't join them. They could hear him rummaging about upstairs. Mrs Macdonald went up to have a word with him. She told him to pull himself together. It was Jojo's big day too. Mouse must not spoil the party!

Mouse went
slowly downstairs.
But he was still worried
about Ricky and furious with
Jojo, and she was annoyed with
him too.

One way and another, the party
got off to a pretty bad start.

Chapter Three

The Treasure Hunt

Mr Macdonald had organised a treasure hunt.
Everyone was delighted. But Mouse didn't want
to look for treasure. He wanted to look for Ricky.
He only agreed to join in when his mum and dad
promised to look for Ricky while he was away.

The first clue was on the washing line.

Over a fence
and round a bend,
get the next clue
from Sam's little friend.

13

The children climbed over the fence and stood at the edge of the park. Who was Sam's little friend?

"Little friends would be in the play area," said Jojo. She started off, but Ben called her back.

"That's not round a bend," he said. "It's round a corner."

"The path bends round towards the bridge," said Ravi. They all shot off together.

Sam stopped to say hello to Mrs Green. She gave Scrap a pat. There was a label tied to his collar. Mrs Green grinned at her.

"I've got it!" Sam called to the others. They screeched to a stop on the bridge, and came running back.

They crowded round to read the clue.

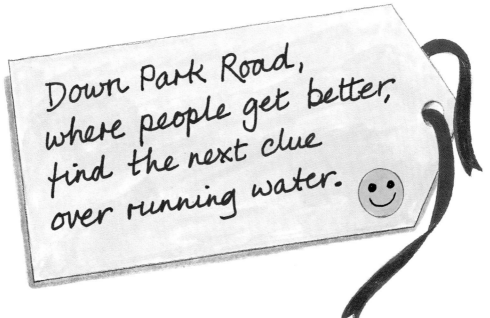

Down Park Road,
where people get better,
find the next clue
over running water. ☺

15

The friends raced off towards Park Road. They knew the clue would be near the hospital.

Suddenly Mouse had a worrying thought. What if Ricky had got out and wandered into the park?

The next clue was written in chalk on the bridge.

FIND A ZEBRA,
THEN HAVE A LOOK
WHERE YOU GO
TO GET A BOOK.

17

"A zebra?" said Billy, scratching his head.
They wandered back towards Story Street.

Then Mouse had another
worrying thought.
What if Ricky was ill?

The others reached the corner.

"There's the zebra!" Sam exclaimed, pointing
to the school crossing.

"You get books in the library," cried Ben.

There was a display of book covers in the library
window and there, in the middle, was the clue.

It was such an easy clue, they all set off at a gallop.

But Mouse couldn't bear it any more. What if Ricky had been kidnapped?

He **had** to find Ricky!

Chapter Four

Jojo and Mouse Do a Deal

The others were outside the shop, when they saw Mouse going across the road towards his house.

"Where are you going?" shouted Jojo.

"I've got to find Ricky!" Mouse thought, what if Ricky has fallen down the toilet? Can rats swim?

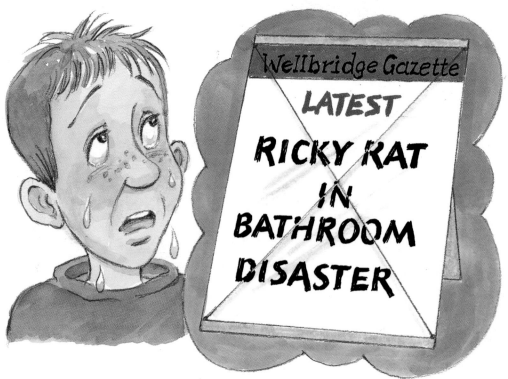

When Jojo saw how worried he was, she stopped feeling so annoyed. "Let's do a deal," she said. "You try to enjoy the rest of the treasure hunt, and then we'll help you look for Ricky. I'm sure we'll find him, with so many of us."

They went back to the others just
as Ben discovered the next clue.

BOOK CLUB
in the school library

Come and
hear
Mick tell us
a story

Every Thursday
from 4.00pm

10.00am – 4.00pm
City Farm, School Lane

A red beast with
a deafening wail,
the clue is
underneath its tail.

24

"This is a hard one," Ben remarked.

"Are there any red animals in the City Farm?" asked Sam.

An ambulance went by, with its siren blaring. They put their hands over their ears.

"That was a deafening wail," said Ravi.

"But an ambulance isn't red," Ben pointed out.

"A fire engine is!" exclaimed Donut.

They were off again.

Mouse thought, what if Ricky has got into the fireplace? But he put the thought firmly out of his mind.

There was a fire engine parked outside the fire station. The hose was spread out behind it like a tail, and the clue was chalked next to it.

Now your quest is nearly done, go back to where it was begun.

They ran back to Mouse and Jojo's house.
There was a note on the door.

Well done!
You've passed the test!
The treasure is here,
so look for a chest.

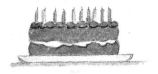

Chapter Five

Finding the Treasure

Sam looked closely at Mr Macdonald's chest as they went in, but he didn't seem to have anything stuffed up his jumper. Where would they find a chest in the Macdonalds' house?

"I know ... the blanket chest!" said Jojo. But the only thing in the blanket chest was blankets.

"What about Pip's toy chest?" suggested Donut. But the only thing in his toy chest was toys.

The friends went downstairs. "There aren't any other chests," they said.

Suddenly Billy gave a shout.

In the freezer, they found a box marked

TREASURE.

It was full of fancy choc-ices wrapped in
gold foil. Jojo handed them round.
"That was brilliant fun," she said.
But Mouse couldn't stand it any more.
"Where's Ricky?" he wailed.

"I know where Ricky is!" said Mrs Macdonald. "I searched high and low for him, and then I thought, where would Ricky most like to be?"

"The food!" cried Mouse. He ran to the table.

"Then I listened for a moment," said his mum. "And I heard a tiny noise."

They all stopped talking and listened. They heard a tiny snuffle and a snore. It was coming from the cake.

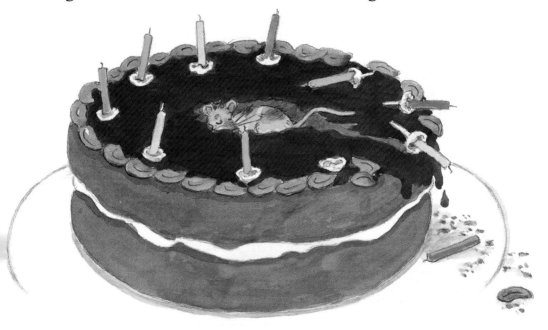

Mouse picked up the plate. There was Ricky, curled up inside the cake, covered in crumbs.

"Oh, no!" cried Jojo.

"Oh, yes!" cried Mouse.

Very delicately, Mouse lifted the rat out and put him on his hand. "This is my treasure," he murmured.

"Oh, yuk!" said Jojo. "Fetch the sick bucket!" But she was glad that Mouse had found him. Everyone laughed, even Mouse. "I'm so happy Ricky's all right that I don't mind about my birthday cake at all," he said.

"It was my cake too," muttered Jojo.

"Next year, perhaps you should have two parties and two cakes," Mum said. "But in the meantime, let's make the best of this last shared party, shall we?"

And they did.